First published in 2006 by
Miles Kelly Publishing Ltd
Bardfield Centre, Great Bardfield, Essex, CM7 4SL

Copyright © Miles Kelly Publishing Ltd 2006

2 4 6 8 10 9 7 5 3 1

Publishing Director:
Anne Marshall

Editor:
Belinda Gallagher

Art Director:
Jo Brewer

Designer:
Louisa Leitao

Cartoons:
Mark Davis

Production:
Elizabeth Brunwin

ISBN 1–84236–658–0

Reprographics: Mike Coupe, Stephan Davis

Printed in China

British Library Cataloguing–in–Publication Data
A catalogue record for this book is available from the British Library

Indexer: Jane Parker

www.mileskelly.net
info@mileskelly.net

AB		MO	
MA		MR	
MB		MT	
MC		MW	
MD			
ME			
MG			
MH			
MM			
MN			

Contents

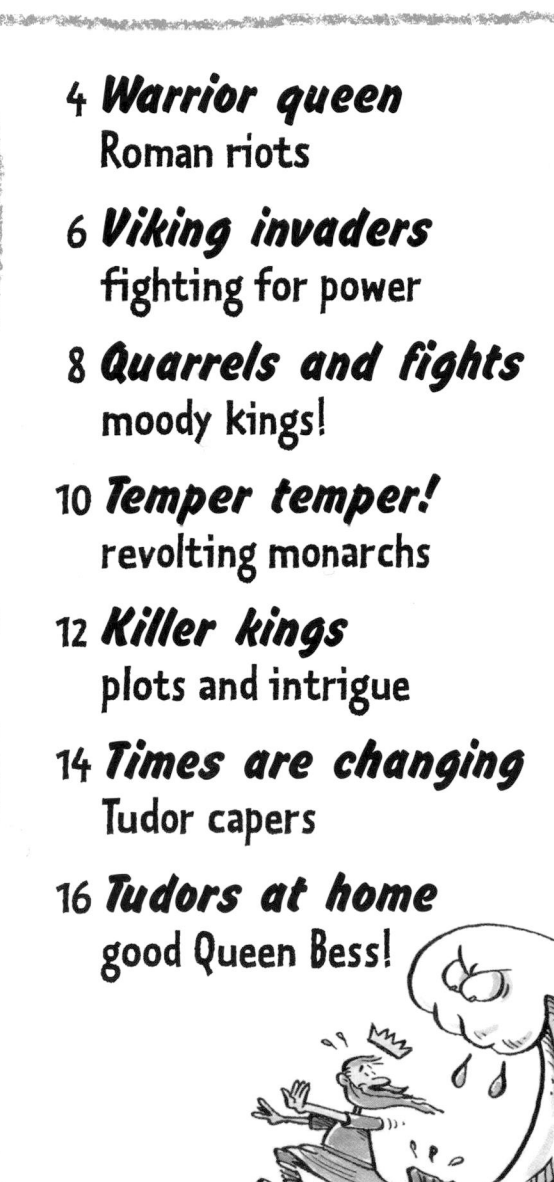

Warrior queen

Roman riots

Queen Boudicca rebelled against the Romans. In AD61, she led an army of Celtic tribes to attack Roman towns. After several Celtic successes, the Romans fought back and defeated the Celts. Rather than surrender, Queen Boudicca took deadly poison and died.

Can you believe it?

The Celts were show-offs! Warriors sometimes wore their hair in spikes, tattoed their skin and wore gold jewellery!

When they stormed a Celtic fort, the Roman army would often form a 'tortoise'. This formation was made by soldiers lifting their shields above their heads. Spears and rocks thrown by the enemy would bounce off the tortoise 'shell'.

The Romans were stopped in their tracks for a while. They eventually fought back and defeated the Celts.

Viking invaders
fighting for power

Cnut the Great was a powerful Viking ruler. He was king of Denmark, Norway and England from 1016 to 1035. Although he was harsh, Cnut claimed to be a good Christian. He used his power as king to bring peace, which lasted until he died.

King Cnut tried to command the waves. Eric Bloodaxe was ruler of York. Enemies forced him to leave.

Sigurd the Stout ruled many Scottish islands between AD985 and 1014. He had a flag with a picture of a raven on it, which he thought would always make him victorious in battle. But Sigurd was eventually defeated.

In 1165, Malcolm IV of Scotland died because he went without food to show his devotion to God.

IT IS A MAGIC FLAG. IT IS, IT IS IT IS!

YEAH OK!!

LONG HAIR IS BANNED!

PITY BIG MOUTHS AREN'T!

Sigurd the Stout thought a flag was magic. Thorfinn the Mighty planned new ways to rule the Orkney Islands.

Quarrels and fights — moody kings!

Henry II was strong and very determined. He passed many strict laws – but he couldn't make his wife, Eleanor of Aquitaine, obey him! In 1173 she led a rebellion against her husband because of the way he was ruling her family's lands in France. Henry imprisoned her for life.

YOU NEED A SMALLER SIZE.

LOCK HER UP... FOREVER!

CHARMING!

THAT'S A BIT EXTREME! NO NEED TO BE SO HASTY!

SWISH! SWISH!

Henry II sent his wife to prison. He argued with Thomas Becket, a Church leader, who was then murdered.

Richard the Lionheart was cruel to his enemies. John I had to sign a document giving people more rights.

Henry III owned Britain's first zoo. He spent his last years planning a new cathedral – Westminster Abbey.

Temper temper!

revolting monarchs

Edward I was the tallest king. He was given the nickname 'Longshanks' meaning long legs, as he was over 2 metres tall! Edward was also very hot-tempered. He once tore out his son's hair in a fury and broke his daughter's coronet!

Edward I had a furious temper. The wife of Edward II was nicknamed 'She-wolf'! She ran away to France.

can you believe it?

When Edward I was stabbed with a poisoned dagger, people say that his wife saved him by sucking out the poison.

In 1348 a terrible disease called the Black Death reached England. Victims developed a cough, high fever and boils on their bodies. Almost half the population of England died. At the time, no one knew what caused the disease. Today, we know that it was caused by rat fleas.

TOO YOUNG TO RIDE INTO BATTLE! PHEW!

FIRE!

PING!

NOT AS EASY AS IT LOOKS...

SPLUTTER!

The Hundred Years War between England and France was started by Edward III. Richard II was a teenage king!

Killer kings

plots and intrigue

Edward IV was a brave fighter. He became king in 1461 and proved to be a clever army commander and politician. But Edward could be ruthless. In his search for power he gave orders for Henry VI to be murdered. When he suspected his brother of plotting against him, he ordered for him to be drowned.

KING IN TRAINING!

CHICKEN SARNIE?

I SAID DIAMONDS!

I MAY BE KING BUT I'M NOT MADE OF MONEY.

YOU'LL LOVE IT IN THE TOWER...

YEAH RIGHT!

Edward IV liked food, drink and pretty women. When he died, his sons were put in the Tower of London.

Richard III died in battle in 1485. He wore his crown as he fought, and was an easy target for the enemy.

Bad stories about Richard III may have been written by Sir Thomas More, who worked for the Tudors.

Times are changing

Tudor capers

Henry VII founded a new ruling family – the Tudors. He was the son of a Welsh lord and an English noblewoman. Although Henry had only a weak claim to be king, after killing Richard III in battle, he brought peace to England.

THIS PEN IS RUBBISH!

I AM THE KING, HONEST.

HMM, YOU LOOK MORE LIKE MY UNCLE HARRY...

WHO?

HE'S AN IMPOSTER!

Henry VII united England. When he died in 1509 the country was richer than it had been for many years.

Henry VIII had six wives. He wanted a son, so he divorced or beheaded many wives until he had his heir.

Henry formed his own church and closed many monasteries. He also set up the first modern navy.

Tudors at home

good Queen Bess!

Elizabeth I decided not to get married. Her mother was Anne Boleyn, the second wife of Henry VIII – and the first to be beheaded. Not getting married meant that Elizabeth didn't have to share her power. When she died in 1603, the Tudor line came to an end.

KEEP YOUR CROWN ON!

C'MON BOYS, SOCK IT TO 'EM!

I DON'T DO MARRIAGE!

IT'S A FLOWER, NOT A RING!

TO WHO?

DUNNO.

Elizabeth I refused to marry. In 1588 she gave a speech to her troops when a Spanish fleet attacked.

Stormin' Normans!

conquest!

In 1066 William the Conqueror killed King Harold at the Battle of Hastings. William was from Normandy in France. He began to build castles as soon as he was king.

The Normans built simple 'motte and bailey' castles. Each had a wooden tower, standing on a tall earth mound called a 'motte'. This was then surrounded by a tall wooden fence. Early castles were used as army bases.

Workers dug a deep ditch called a moat around the outside of the castle, to stop attackers getting in.

The first castles were brought to England by sea. The Normans made them in sections from wood, before they invaded in 1066. These were then loaded onto their battle ships. When they arrived in England, the Normans put the castles together.

For extra protection the wooden planks that made up the fence were sharpened into points.

When a king lost... his head!

James VI and James I were the same man! Already the sixth king of Scotland, James became the first king to rule both England and Scotland. He ruled each country separately – the two did not become a united kingdom until 1707.

James hated smoking and wrote a book about its dangers. But he was foolishly fond of some silly friends.

Charles I thought he was chosen by God to be king. But he argued with Parliament and started a civil war.

The Roundheads supported Parliament and the Cavaliers supported the king. In 1648 Charles was executed.

Although German, George I had a claim to the English throne. He also preferred to speak German or French. King of England, Scotland and Wales from 1714 to 1727, George was the great grandson of James I. He also locked his wife, Dorothea, away in a castle when she became friends with a handsome nobleman.

MUST GET A NEW WIG.

NO CHANCE!

DINNER?

GOOD RIDDANCE!

OH NO!

SPLAT

George I was furious with his wife, and locked her up. Riding into battle in 1743, George II fell off his horse!

can you believe it?

George II died while visiting the closet (royal lavatory). He collapsed from a heart attack and died there.

Bonnie Prince Charlie was called the 'Young Pretender'. He claimed to be the rightful English and Scottish king. When he invaded Scotland in 1745 his attack went well. His army marched towards London but was forced to retreat by the English soldiers. After the Battle of Culloden, Charlie spent many weeks in hiding until Flora MacDonald helped him to escape.

Bonnie Prince Charlie's army was massacred by the English at the Battle of Culloden in 1746.

By George!

mad and bad

George III wanted to be a farmer. He lived during the Agricultural Revolution. This was a time when farmers were experimenting with new crops, techniques and machinery. George ruled from 1760 to 1820. His long reign saw rebellions in America and Ireland and a war with France.

George III liked to talk to the people. But he had spells of mental illness and would talk to trees!

George IV loved drinking, wearing nice clothes – and eating fine food. He didn't take his duties seriously.

In 1830, Parliament wanted to let the people vote. William IV said no, and earned the nickname Silly Billy.

Bring on the Victorians

empire builders

Queen Victoria ruled the largest empire in the world. She became queen in 1837 and ruled for 64 years. During her reign Britain became a world leader in technology. The arrival of steam-powered ships and locomotives allowed people to travel further afield than ever before.

Queen Victoria married Prince Albert and had nine children. Steam engines helped to transport goods.

Queen Victoria became known as the 'grandmother of Europe'. Because Britain was so powerful, many other European countries wanted to show friendship. So they arranged marriages between Victoria's children and their own.

Like many other British people, Queen Victoria became fascinated by India's cultural heritage and rich civilization. She collected Indian jewels and art treasures and hired an Indian servant to teach her one of India's languages, Hindi.

WHAT D'YA THINK?

I THINK IT'S A BRIDGE...

AATCHOOO! DARNED FEATHERS!

RULE BRITANNIA!

Amazing bridges and architecture were built in Victoria's reign. The queen became empress of India, too.

Wartime royals

stiff upper lip!

After Queen Victoria died, her son became king as Edward VII. His reign lasted from 1901 until 1910, and Edward proved to be a skilled politician and diplomat. He also spoke many foreign languages very well.

Edward VII also had a fun side and he liked fast cars, horse racing, gambling and sailing.

George V saw the outbreak of World War I in 1914. Edward VIII gave up his throne for love.

George VI didn't want to be king. London was bombed during World War II, but the royals didn't leave.

Modern times

Elizabeth II

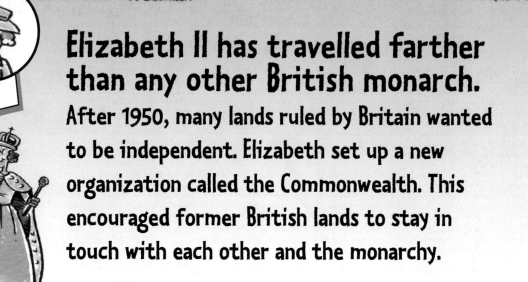

Elizabeth II has travelled farther than any other British monarch. After 1950, many lands ruled by Britain wanted to be independent. Elizabeth set up a new organization called the Commonwealth. This encouraged former British lands to stay in touch with each other and the monarchy.

Queen Elizabeth II has travelled thousands of miles meeting other Commonwealth people and leaders.

can you believe it?

George IV was very fat! This earned him the nickname 'Prince of Whales' when he was Prince Regent!

Elizabeth married Prince Philip in 1947. They have four children – Princes Charles, Andrew and Edward – and Princess Anne. When Prince Philip married, one of the new titles he was given was Duke of Edinburgh.

NICE HAT. IS IT NEW?

BLESS YOU, MY CHILD.

I HATE QUEUES. CAN'T WE PUSH TO THE FRONT?

CHEATS!

Prince Philip is Queen Elizabeth's husband. He has accompanied her on many of her travels to foreign lands.

Index